THE AUTHORITY GUIDE TO PUBLISHING YOUR BUSINESS BOOK

Take your business to a new level by becoming an authority in your field

SUE RICHARDSON

The Authority Guide to Publishing your Business Book

Take your business to a new level by becoming an authority in your field

ISBN 9781909116795
eISBN 9781909116801

Published in 2016 by Authority Guides
authorityguides.co.uk

A CIP record of this book is available from the British Library.

Printed in the United Kingdom.

Thank yous

The fabulous team at SRA, Kelly Mundt, Ian Hunter, Maria Waite – superstars all of you. William Buist for continually asking me great questions. Melissa Tredinnick for her help with the research for this book. I could not do any of it without you guys – the next round is forever on me at The Orchard.

Thank you too to all the authors who shared their experience and book recommendations so enthusiastically. Your generosity has been truly humbling.

And last, but by no means least, thank you to my incredible parents, Pat and Giles Harbottle. It's thanks to you that I was blessed from a very early age with a passion for words and books.

“

Man's Search for Meaning: The classic tribute to hope from the Holocaust
by Viktor E. Frankl (Rider, 2004)

Because it helped me to realise that I am able to control how I feel and how I respond to every situation, and that any excuses I have are pathetic.

David Hyner
professional speaker
author of ***Stress Management: How not to be the richest person in the graveyard***

”

Contents

The New Psycho-Cybernetics: The original science of self-improvement and success that has changed the lives of 30 million people by Maxwell Maltz (Prentice Hall Press, 2003)

I read this some time late 2004. I was going through a crisis in confidence and someone recommended it to me. It helped me to understand what was going on in my head and how to deal with it to get back on track. I applied and refined the information to grow my business and even used the same insights and tools to effectively lose 7st (98 lbs, 45 kg) in excess weight. Not only did it help me get my head straight and focused, it became the foundation of my career and the keynote speeches I deliver today at conferences and events on Achievement Thinking which I apply to resilience, managing change and success mindset.

John Hotowka
Achievement Thinking speaker
(www.hotowka.co.uk)

Introduction

How to Win Friends and Influence People by Dale Carnegie (Vermilion, 2006)

The book would be *How to Win Friends and Influence People* by Dale Carnegie as it helped me understand the importance of building relationships with people. Whatever line of work you are in, relationships are crucial to success and this book inspired me several years after reading it, to write my own book *How to Succeed with People*.

Paul McGee
author of ***How to Succeed with People: Remarkably easy ways to engage, influence and motivate almost anyone***

Introduction

So you're good at what you do. You've been doing it a long time. You've studied the books, you've sweated the detail, you've really learned your stuff. You've helped dozens or even hundreds of people throughout your career by advising them and guiding them on to the right path. You know you can help a lot more people, solving their problems, getting them to where they want to be. Yet you're not the only one out there. There are others shooting for the stars, looking to take the position of 'go-to' person in your field or business in your market.

So how can you compete?

We live in an ever faster paced, constantly shifting world. Innovations bring opportunities like never before, and yet the noise out there can be deafening. Choosing the experts to help them find their way becomes more and more crucial for every business, big or small. In some cases this choice could even have a bearing on the survival or demise of the business.

As an expert in your world, how can you make sure it's *you* they find? How will the chief executive officer (CEO) choose *you* to call on the day when they are faced with a threat to the future of their business?

Establishing authority and credibility and gaining the trust of your peers, your people and your customers is key. You need to demonstrate you have deep expertise derived from experience and the application of knowledge.

You might do this by talking to the press, writing columns and articles, or producing a great regular blog and a content-rich website.

Or you could write and publish a book.

'If blogs are the kings of valuable content, business books are the Masters of the Universe', say Sonja Jefferson and Sharon Tanton in their book *Valuable Content Marketing* (2015).

And they are right, as I hope to demonstrate in these pages.

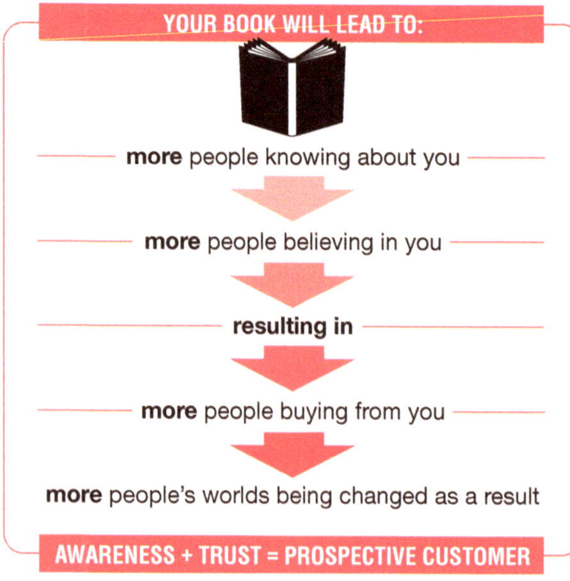

Many business books are published every year and there is little doubt that many of them end up not doing the job the authors dreamed they would do.

In this book my aim is to help you to avoid the pitfalls of publishing a bad book, or the wrong book. Each of the next four chapters looks at a specific aspect of creating and publishing a book.

- Why publish a business book? What will the book do for you?
- Who is it for? What will it do for them?
- What should you write?
- How should you publish it?

Of course, as with any product, the marketing of your book is crucial. However, although thinking about your target market is covered in Who should you write for and how will your book reach them?, I do not cover in detail the 'how-to' of this important aspect. Please refer to our sister publication *The Authority Guide to Marketing Your Business Book* by book public relations (PR) and publicist, Chantal Cooke, for her expert advice.

At the end of each of the four chapters there is a 'Time to commit' section, where I encourage you to make some decisions about the why, the who, the what and the how of publishing your book, and write these down. If you do this you should find by the end you have the bones of a publishing plan.

“

Influence: Science and practice by Robert Cialdini (Pearson, 2008)

There is one book I come back to time and time again and use his practices on my workshops both in what I do, and also pass the tips on to others, and that's Robert Cialdini's *Influence: Science and practice*.

Kate Atkin
author of ***The Confident Manager***

”

Why publish a business book?

Mavericks at Work: Why the most original minds in business win by William Taylor (Harper, 2011)

Mavericks at work reminded me that it is not only possible to be different, but positively wonderful to be so. Reading about very different ways of working, very different ways of building culture contributed to creating NearDesk and DeskLodge.

Tom Ball
CEO, NearDesk

Why publish a business book?

'Here's the thing: The book that will most change your life is the book you write.'

Seth Godin

In preparing to write this book, I approached several established and respected authors of business books with the question: 'What has publishing a book done for you/your business?' I received many fascinating answers and have shared these valuable insights from those who have walked their talk throughout the book.

This is the answer I got from Paul McGee, author of *S.U.M.O (Shut Up, Move On)*:

> Publishing books for me has had a profound and significant impact on my business. When my book was published in May 2005 it became WHSmith business book of the month. It's gone on to sell over 125,000 copies worldwide and has literally provided me with opportunities to speak around the world. It's opened doors that I wasn't even pushing and this along with my other books, will be part of my legacy.

Over the years, others have talked to me about how their book has turned them into a magnet, started the phone ringing off the hook and caused their marketing to change completely from push to pull. Imagine never having to make a sales call again. Imagine if your inbox was full of enquiries inviting you to speak at conferences or write articles. Imagine you could be in hundreds of rooms at once, imparting your ideas and your expertise for the benefit of others.

The most successful authors I have worked with have been those that have been very clear from the start about their objectives for publishing in the first place. Over the past 20 years of helping authors get published, I have come to recognise that the clearer the author is about their reasons for publishing, the more likely they are to succeed.

I sum these objectives up as 'the 7 pearls of publishing':

- Purpose/passion
- Profit
- Presence
- Protection
- Profile
- PR
- Purple Cow (Seth Godin)

Insight from a business book author

Sonja Jefferson, content marketing consultant and trainer and co-author (with Sharon Tanton) of *Valuable Content Marketing: How to make quality content your key to success*

A book changes things.

It definitely does.

The first edition of *Valuable Content Marketing* came out in 2013 and the second in 2015. SO much has happened as a result.

Firstly, writing the book helped me to unpick and codify the Valuable Content approach. I think this has made us better at what we do. It has also helped us shift our business model in a more sustainable (and happier) direction – from pure consultancy to a digital marketing school for small business owners. Big change.

We create a lot of content for our clients – blogs, newsletters, videos, ebooks – but the book is the most valuable content of all, the jewel in the crown. I love it when clients and others tell me how useful they've found it, how it's inspired them to take action and helped them grow their business as a result.

The book has flown out into the world and pulled great people towards us – it's attracted some amazing clients and new business friends. It's physically taken us a long way – we've delivered talks and workshops from London to Lanzarote to Chicago (as well as in our local pub) on the back of that book. It even helped to attract the attention of Google! We're a two woman business in Bristol, and we never expected to be helping the world's most valuable company to create ever more valuable content. It's opened doors we never expected to walk through, that's for sure.

Sharon and I wrote the first book together before we became business partners. We survived the process (just!) and came out smiling. The perfect test to see if we could build a business together. And we have.

Writing the *Valuable Content Marketing* book has helped us to create a better business – one we're really proud to run. Not an easy thing to do, but definitely worth it.

Pearl 1: purpose/passion

> Imagine if every organization started with WHY. Decisions would be simpler. Loyalties would be greater. Trust would be a common currency… No matter the size of the organization, no matter the industry, no matter the product or the service, if we all take some responsibility to start with WHY and inspire others to do the same, then, together, we can change the world.
>
> Simon Sinek, *Start with Why* (2011)

Speaking as I do to dozens of authors every year about what has driven them to write, it's clear to me that those who make the decision to put their knowledge in a book are the most focused of individuals. Often entrepreneurial by nature, authors of business books tend to have a burning ambition to get their message to a wide audience. They are usually very passionate about what they do and their passion creates energy, the petrol in their tanks, getting them up in the morning and keeping them going through the hard times that all business owners face.

The sort of phrases I hear authors come up with are:

- 'I want to make a difference.'
- 'My ideas could change people's lives.'
- 'I'm on a mission to change the world.'
- 'I believe I have something important to share.'

Changing the world doesn't have to mean being a Mother Theresa or a Martin Luther King. It doesn't even necessarily mean attaining massive celebrity or a position of power. We are all capable of changing the world around us in smaller ways. Creating a great business that employs people and helps them to build happy, successful lives is just one example. Or you may end up as a professional speaker, getting your message to a roomful of people at a time, or even a global audience online via a TED talk. Even if one person changes the way they think, and does something constructive as a result, you will have made a significant difference.

Books have the power to change people's lives and therefore the world. I vividly remember reading Michael Gerber's *E-Myth Revisited* and realising that I could no longer stand in the shadows as a freelance editor and that I needed to step into a different way of looking at things and become a publishing entrepreneur. Many people I know have had similarly powerful lessons from the same book or others like it. Throughout this book you will find examples of books that people who are authorities in their fields have been influenced by. We all love to share recommendations in this way.

Now, imagine a future where it's *your* book that is being recommended and the word is being passed by someone whose life *you* have changed.

Passion may create energy, but another great reason for writing a book is that it helps you to focus on what it is that you are actually passionate about. Many business owners have been in business for a long time, and some may have lost their way to the extent that they are no longer 100 per cent sure what they are in business for.

We love to read books by other business leaders – millions of them sell every year. We find these stories inspiring and motivating. How will your story help to stir the passion in the hearts of potentially successful entrepreneurs like you?

What is your mission or purpose? What are you truly passionate about? It helps to get really clear about this before you start to write your book as it will help you to get the right book written.

Ask yourself the questions:

- What am I in business for?
- What is my life's purpose?
- How will what I do change the world?

Insight from a business book author

Graham Jones, author of *Clickology: What works in online shopping and how your business can use consumer psychology to succeed, Sales Genius: 40 insights from the science of selling* and many other business titles.

Writing business books has been of significant help to my business. People will tell you all about the fact that being an author adds credibility and authority to your name and your business. However, I believe that writing business books has other, possibly more important, effects on your business.

A book needs to be well organised and engaging. Writing a book means you have to really think about your topic. I often meet business people who have no real idea about what they do in business, or who they do it for. When I ask what they do, all they tell me is their profession – accountant, lawyer, marketer, for instance. But that doesn't explain things. If these people had written a book it would have forced them to think. Otherwise, their book would have been so general and lacking focus that no-one would read it. Writing a book ensures that you have thought about your topic and that you have focused your mind on what you can help other people achieve. Writing a book makes you a better business person because of this.

There are also other somewhat hidden effects of being an author. Book editors are fastidious at checking everything;

they nit-pick all day long. When your book goes off to be edited you will soon get challenged by the editor. You will be asked to justify the claims you make and you will be pushed for evidence to support what you say in the book. The editorial process makes a business person much more professional. No longer can you get away with saying the same old things; the book editors force you into making sure that what you say is accurate, fair, and honest. Their challenges make you better at business overall because you start to question everything you say.

Finally, there is another benefit of writing a business book and that is in helping to improve your communications ability. Many people in business are notoriously bad at communicating; they say one thing, but mean another. Writing a book will force you to be clear; the writing and editing processes help business people to become better communicators.

So, overall, writing business books has helped me establish credibility and authority in my sector. But more than this it has helped me understand what I really offer people by focusing my mind. It has made sure that I strive for accuracy in everything I do. Plus, I am confident it has improved my communication skills. Even if no-one actually read any of my books, those benefits would have been worth it for my business.

Pearl 2: profit

In recent years there has been a huge rise in the number of owners of service-led businesses perceiving the need to create products in order to develop value and profit. While this strategy may turn out to be lucrative for many, in my experience it rarely pays off if the product is a book.

There are several reasons for this. First, the profit margin on books is generally small. Second, with the odd exception, unlike books by celebrity chefs or some fiction authors, business books simply don't sell in large enough numbers.

To take the first reason, if you self-publish your book (see How should you publish?) you may receive as much as 40 per cent of the cover price from Amazon, but you will also have the costs of shipping to pay out. If your book is traditionally published you will be lucky to receive 8–10 per cent of the net receipts of the publisher – which equates to around 4–5 per cent of the cover price.

If you sell 1,000 a books in a year you will be doing very well – so with the average trade discounts and/or Amazon commissions you may break even in your first year and make a small profit in your second year.

Now, if you are an entrepreneurial type, you may well be beginning to feel a little hot under the collar about these sort of figures. Well, I'm here to tell you to relax!

In fact, I believe quite firmly that it's not in the pounds, shillings and pence that your profits from book sales lie. While books themselves may not always make lots of money in terms of actual product sales, as a marketing tool they are second to none.

Many years ago I worked with a marketing company to produce a small book for their client, a local family law firm. The small book they created contained articles about different aspects of family law, each chapter being written by a specialist in their area who was a partner in the firm. The marketer who came up with the concept for them told me she had recently met a woman who had not been very happy in her marriage and who had, at some point, come into contact with the law firm and been given the little book. She had carried that book around in her handbag for several months. When the crunch came and she needed help, who else would she have turned to? There was the book in her bag, full of helpful information and evidence of the authority of the law firm that created it.

Insight from a business book author

Bryony Thomas, CEO of Watertight Marketing and author of *Watertight Marketing: Delivering long-term sales results*

For me the business plan came before the book and the book is at the heart of that business. Watertight Marketing is essentially an end-to-end methodology captured in a book. I had already been using this process with individual clients but, publishing it as a book, has allowed me to move from the classic consulting time-for-money business model into something scalable.

From having a best-selling book, I have now been able to successfully license the intellectual property with a growing network of independent marketing consultants, accredited by me to use my materials with their clients.

In addition, the nature of the material lends itself perfectly to a structured programme which I deliver in both online and offline one to many contexts.

Writing *Watertight Marketing* has moved my business to a completely different place. Much more than just a business card, *Watertight Marketing* is a manual, a methodology and a mindset. Authors who truly want to put a book at the heart of their business need the business plan before they write the book.

I've met many authors who've said they want to focus on becoming a number one bestseller on Amazon or that they want to get their book reviewed in the business pages. I've seen a lot of time, money and energy being wasted in an attempt to get people to buy books. Take a close look at your strategy and see whether you really should prioritise product sales over simply getting your book in front of as many people as you can. As many of our business authors have mentioned in their insights in this book, a book can be a lasting reminder of your expertise and authority. So, while profit may be a very important objective for you, I recommend that you think of it coming from the other benefits a book brings, rather than just from sales of the book product.

Pearl 3: presence

This simple pearl is key to the magical properties of books. By becoming a published author you are suddenly able to be in many places at one time.

My good friend and business mentor, William Buist, said to me recently that he believed that the definition of authority was when other people talked about you behind your back – in a good way!

A well-written, insightful, authoritative book will allow you to be talked about by others. How many times have you been at a business meeting and had a book recommended to you by a colleague, while discussing either a problem or a business issue?

You may well be a good speaker, or an effective networker. You may write a blog and comment on social media regularly. All of this is great for creating presence. Imagine also having a small army of books, marching out to spread your message to an even wider audience. Books that will be placed in other people's hands because they have helped. Books that hold your name, your business credentials and your authority within them.

Another type of presence is the online one that is created when you publish a book. Amazon is a highly searched website in its own right and also, because of its rich content, delivers great results in Google too. Google Books also catalogues all book content – so the chances of your book appearing in search results are very high, and increasing all the time.

Insight from a business book author

Alan Stevens, The Media Coach and author of *The Exceptional Speaker*, *Ping*, *MediaMasters* and many other business titles.

A business book is a validation of your business credibility. Being able to give a physical object that confirms my expertise to a potential client has been the best business card I have ever had. Not only that, it creates a lasting reminder that sits on your client's shelf and catches their eye from time to time. That's when they give you a call. Writing a business book is one of the best things a business authority can do.

Pearl 4: protection

No, I'm not talking about some kind of Mafia style extortion racket here. However, it is true to say that if you have a great idea in business, very soon someone else will take your idea and do something with it to further their own ends.

Great ideas spread and in time it is possible that, no matter how good your idea, people will forget that it was you that came up with it.

A key objective for many business authors is the absolute stamp of ownership that a book gives them. If you write it down in a book and publish it properly, your words will be protected by copyright law. That means that no one else can use your words or your graphics unless you grant permission to them to do so. Hence your ideas are, to some extent, protected.

There really isn't a better way to do this that I can think of.

Insight from a business book author

Andy Lopata, networking guru and author of *Recommended* and *...and Death Came Third!*

One of the main benefits of authoring books for me has been getting my IP (intellectual property) into print and thereby marking key content as originating from me.

We are all encouraged to be 'thought leaders'. The mere suggestion that you are a 'leader' implies that others will follow.

When I classed myself as a 'business networking strategist', there were very few people I was aware of worldwide using the term. Now it is commonplace, at least 'networking strategy' is. I don't get defensive about that, I take it as a compliment and an indication that I was on the right path.

I don't, however, want to be seen as derivative of others when, in fact, I would argue that I innovated in many areas. Of course, I wasn't the first to talk about a number of areas I cover but I always try to credit my sources. Not everyone does that.

A book is one way of laying down your marker. Demonstrating what you are sharing and when. It has more credibility, a longer and greater impact than a blog or article and greater reach and stickiness than a speech.

Pearl 5: profile

The higher your profile in the business world, the more people will come to you to buy, and the more money you can charge them for working with them. If you are an authority in your field, it will pay you to make sure that more people know about you. A book helps you with that, as we've seen earlier, but it also builds credibility. The fact is that if you've written a book people accept that you have a good solid amount of knowledge and expertise in its subject. They will be impressed, whether they read it or not.

There are many ways these days to raise your profile – perhaps the most common one being on social media platforms. However, these can be quite a minefield as you jostle with other experts who may have discovered better ways to engage with bigger crowds.

The big differentiator, whether we are looking at Twitter, Facebook, LinkedIn, or increasingly YouTube and Instagram, is when the expert has also published a book. Being an author can make you the 'go-to' person in your field if you make sure you use it correctly.

Insight from a business book author

Robert Craven, CEO of The Director's Centre and author of *Grow your Service Firm* and *Grow your Digital Agency*

Before

- Starting to write a book helps you to get all your thoughts in order.
- The book writing process helps you simplify your message and focus on key points.
- The submission of a book proposal makes you write a 'business plan' identifying your target audience, their hurts and how you can help them.
- The mere process of committing to write the book shows you that you are serious about your trade as a communicator of your own ideas.

During

- Writing makes you realise exactly how much of your material is your own as opposed to 'borrowed' from other sources.
- Writing is a discipline that helps you understand how your ideas fit together and how they can help your audience.
- Just like teaching someone how to drive, writing a book makes you have to slow down and see your material from the audience's point of view.

After

- The real work starts when the book is published.
- A book without an audience reminds me of the question 'If you clap in the jungle and there is no-one there to hear the clap, did the clap ever exist?'

- It's only when you get feedback from people you don't know at all that you can start to understand how your ideas help others.
- When it comes to marketing your books, it's up to you to go the extra mile.

Pearl 6: PR

Alongside the credibility from being a published author comes added visibility. Again to echo our 'insighter', Alan Stevens, the book is the most impressive calling card a business owner is likely to have. So who would be the most important people to impress in order to gain the maximum visibility possible?

Journalists love books. Journalists love authors. Authors have a head start with journalists because they have proved themselves to be an expert simply by having written the book in the first place. The book contains the information they need, the stories are laid out for them. Less digging, less research, less effort.

Take Vicki Wusche, a property investor. As well as having a successful property investment business, she also teaches and mentors other investors. Vicki has been publishing independently since 2010. Her *Using Other People's Money: How to invest in property* is now in its fourth edition. She also published *Make More Money from Property* and *Property for the Next Generation* in 2012. In 2013 she was placed on the list of 'the top 20 most influential people in property' by *The Daily Telegraph*. She has had numerous mentions in that paper as well as in hundreds of other online and print publications. Her business has grown exponentially as a result.

All of this came about because the journalists loved her books.

Insight from a book publicist and business book author

Chantal Cooke, Panpathic Communications, author of *PR Demystified* and *The Authority Guide to Marketing your Business Book*

Writing a business book is a great way to build your authority – but in order to maximise the benefits you really need to let everyone know about the book! Otherwise – what's the point?

In an ideal world you'd start promoting the book as soon as you type the first words, but we all know that most of us don't live in this ideal world. So just start as soon as you can. Even if it's months after publication – don't let that put you off, get started now, and you can still reap the benefits.

So, in short, it's never too early, or too late, to start promoting your book and using it to build your authority and visibility.

Here are a few examples of clients we have worked with recently. Each one has put time, effort, and resource into promoting their book(s) – and has reaped the benefits of thousands and thousands of pounds of free publicity.

John Reynard came to us before his book was published and between us we put a plan in place to maximise the coverage and leverage it. His book *The Spiritual Route to Entrepreneurial Success: From harassed sole trader to visionary CEO* has received considerable coverage and has helped position John as a thought leader and the go-to person in his new venture 'The School of Spiritual Entrepreneurship'. John was already a successful entrepreneur and had recently sold his business; so he had a template for success. And this included telling as many people as possible about his new book before it was published through print, online and radio coverage.

We started promoting Juliet Grayson's book *Landscapes of the Heart: The working world of a sex and relationship therapist* around the time of publication. The book received so much coverage (including a double page spread in *The Sun*, and a number of features in *GQ*, *The Daily Mail*, *The Mirror*, *Marie Claire*, etc.) that Juliet has now been signed-up by a traditional publisher who has taken on her book.

Joanne Henson approached us long after her books had been published. She wanted to give them a new boost. Her two books *What's Your Excuse For Not Eating Healthily?* and *What's Your Excuse For Not Getting Fit?* generated hundreds of thousands of pounds worth of free coverage. Joanne's authority became so high that people started approaching her asking to be included in her next 'What's your excuse' book.

When you decide to write a book, you need to understand the 'why' – i.e. why are you writing this book, what do you want from it? If the answer is 'I want to reach 1000s of people and build my authority and visibility in my field' then putting time, energy and resource into promoting the book is essential.

Whether you do it yourself, or outsource it to a professional – the key is to do something (or preferably quite a few things!), do them as soon as you can, and keep doing them.

Pearl 7: purple cow

I am shamelessly stealing my seventh pearl of publishing from the great author and thought leader, Seth Godin.

Godin's *Purple Cow* was another life changing business book for me. It was the first time I had really understood the concept of what it took to be remarkable in business, as well as the fact that, in the 21st century, being remarkable wasn't just a good idea, it was crucial.

The fact is that most of us in business hold ourselves too small. We don't want to take centre stage. We hide in the wings and while we believe that we can build great businesses, we don't actually challenge or change anything at all. In truth, most of us can build a business that gives us a decent job and maybe a few others a pay cheque – and in reality that is all we want. And there's nothing wrong with that.

But do you want a little more? Are you looking to be one of the world changers mentioned earlier? If so, a book should be a crucial part of your plan.

To borrow Seth's wisdom, the fact is that most business owners or professionals don't write books about their expertise. So by being one of the few that do, you will make yourself remarkable.

Insight from a business book author

Liz Gooster, former publisher of Financial Times Prentice Hall business books at Pearson and editor-at-large for Kogan Page

As my old boss used to say 'Your book is the biggest and best business card you can get.' Having a book that captures your thinking and knowledge about your area of business expertise establishes your credibility and authority better than almost anything else. Of course it has to be well structured and well written and it has to have a clear message, one that is aligned to your business. It helps if you know your objectives in publishing your book before you start writing it – what do you want your book to achieve for you? What are the most important and valuable messages you can share with readers? What will success look like for you? And finally, get some high quality, professional help with editing and publishing your book. It's hard work to do it all alone and your book reflects your business brand: you can't afford for it not to be the best it can be.

Insight from a business book author

Tim Johnson, author of *The Success Book: How to grow yourself and your business*

The act of writing my book has been one of the most profound personal and professional development experiences I've had – and I've had many...!

It takes you to places to nail your clarity and to realise you knew more than you thought you knew and that the things that you thought you knew you didn't know quite as rigorously as you thought.

And then of course once it's written you realise there is more... But that's another story.

Time to commit

Which of the seven pearls apply to you? Write down, in order of priority, which of them align with your business and personal objectives. Under each pearl write down a few reasons they are important to you. You will be starting to create your book publishing strategy by setting your sights on future success.

Secrets of Successful Speakers: How you can motivate, captivate and persuade by Lilly Walters (McGraw-Hill Education, 1993)

As an entrepreneur and a business speaker that wishes to influence people, I found Lilly Walters' book *Secrets of Successful Speakers* invaluable. It contains the very best recipes from America's best speakers and provides a powerful potion for persuasive presentations.

Stephen Harvard-Davis
business consultant and speaker
author of ***Why do 40% of Executives Fail?: How not to have an executive failure on my hands*** *and* ***Write, Publish and Prosper***

Who should you write for?

“

Differentiate or Die: Survival in our era of killer competition by Jack Trout (John Wiley & Sons, 2008)

The simplicity of the central argument is compelling, and is a great antidote to overly complex marketing philosophy and planning. To win – you simply need to be different from your competitors. This reworking of Rosser Reeve's 'unique selling proposition' is an easy read – and motivates me when business life becomes challenging. I recommend it to anyone who needs a 'pick me up'.

Mike Harris
general manager, Northern Europe, SVP Worldwide,
author of ***Find Your Lightbulb***

”

Who should you write for?

You should now have a good idea of your objectives for publishing a book and an understanding of what can be achieved by pushing ahead with writing. The next important stage of your planning is to understand who you should be writing for.

A book is an influential thing, as we've established, and at its best has the capability of changing the reader's perspective or even their life. Who will your book most influence? Who would you like to reach out to in order to achieve your objectives? If you have a passion to educate people in your field of expertise, who is it who will most benefit? Do the future profits of your business rely on you building relationships with decision makers in a particular industry, and if so can your book help you to do that? Or are you looking to raise your PR profile with journalists so that you end up on the breakfast TV couch?

Reader profiling

Taking your list of prioritised objectives created at the end of Why publish a business book?, have a think about the sort of person you need your book to reach and influence. This will help you to find the right tone and style when you start to write.

If you have already started to write, still do this exercise – you can always edit your work if you find you need to.

A few things to think about:

- What is their occupation?
- Are they managers, and if so at what level of management do they sit in their organisation?
- Are they business owners/leaders themselves, and if so of a start-up, an established small to medium-sized enterprise (SME) or are they CEO of a bigger business?
- Is your audience likely to be made up of more women than men or vice versa?
- Are your readers studying business, and if so are they at school, college or university. Are they at BA or MBA level?
- Are they aspiring to greater things in life and in their business? Are they looking to be inspired or instructed?
- What keeps them awake at night and how will your book help?

The important thing is to be as clear as you can be about your audience so that you write the book for them and not for some invisible group of people that don't actually exist, or worse that you end up writing for no one but yourself.

Writing for a niche

One of the most successful books I have ever worked on was a book for a textile artist who was working with a particular fibre people had heard of but didn't really know how to use. She had been inundated with requests for workshops to show people what to do with it and decided a book would ease the pressure. Her book would never have been taken up by a traditional publisher as they would simply not have recognised the market for it. She ended up selling over 25,000 copies of her self-published book and becoming the world's leading expert in the use of that fibre. This led her to develop a fantastic business teaching globally.

We all know as business owners that a niche is a very good thing. It is easier to market a book to a tiny niche, partly because the people in that niche are often underserved. If no publisher will touch a book that is deliberately aimed at a small number of people, then imagine how that small number of people will leap at the chance to gain the wisdom in your book? So if you are not certain if your audience is big enough, take a long look at it before you widen your book's appeal.

Where in the world?

If you are looking to diversify your business geographically, it also pays to think about where in the world your book needs to reach.

If you want to influence people in India or China, for example, you may want to talk to your publisher to make sure they are likely to have the opportunities to sell rights in that country, so that your name becomes known there.

Even as an independently funded author, it is possible to sell the rights to your book. Another artist I have worked with sold the rights to her book in both the US and Germany during the first year after publication. It's a good idea to really examine the possibilities for reaching a global audience before you start to write – then you can make sure you are delivering something that will sell in the places you want to be seen in.

How will your book reach your readers?

Again, it's a good idea to think this through before deciding on what you are going to write and how you are going to publish.

Later on in How should you publish?, we will look at methods of distribution for books and how the book trade works. For now, think about how you will reach the readers you have identified. People buy books in many different ways. It is true that probably these days most of us will go first to online stores, particularly Amazon. And there is still a large number of people (me included!) who like nothing more than browsing in a good bookshop.

For some authors, neither Amazon nor high street bookshops are relevant. Perhaps your plan is to create the best calling card you've ever had and simply give it away to your clients and prospective clients?

How do you think the majority of your readers will receive a copy of your book?

Another factor to consider is whether your readers will prefer a printed, physical book, an ebook to read on a Kindle, an iPad or a phone, or maybe even choose to listen to your book on an audio device?

Time to commit

If you haven't already done it make a list of the characteristics of your perfect reader. See page 32 for a reminder.

Are you writing for a niche market? How small can you make that niche? List the countries you would like your book to be available in. And finally, write down how your book will reach the readers you've identified and whether they will want digital or physical copies of your book.

What and how should you write?

“

Million Dollar Consulting: The professional's guide to growing a practice by Alan Weiss (McGraw-Hill Education, 5th edn, 2016)

The best book I read to grow my business is *Million Dollar Consulting* by Alan Weiss. I read it at a time when I was doing really well but was searching for new insights and ideas. I found it brilliant for giving a new – and infinitely better – way of viewing consultancy. Best of all: I read it at exactly the right time for my development so was able to implement things immediately.

Andy Bounds
international bestselling author, award-winning consultant and creator of andyboundsonline.com
author of ***The Jelly Effect: How to make your communication stick, The Snowball Effect: Communication techniques to make you unstoppable*** *and* ***Top Dog: Impress and influence everyone you meet***

”

What and how should you write?

As an independent publishing consultant, I am frequently faced with a would-be author who knows quite well that publishing a business book will bring huge benefits to their business. The question foremost in their mind, having made this decision, is 'What should I write?' What kind of book will be right for them and their audience?

Again it really helps to be clear about the two questions that form the premise of the first two chapters of this book. The clearer you are about *why* you are writing your book and *who* the book is for, the easier it will be to decide exactly *what* it is that you should write.

Finding your subject

This should be the straightforward bit. You are an expert at what you do, so it may seem obvious to say that you need to focus on your expertise. You may be surprised to learn that, when working with business owners, I am frequently presented with books that aren't 100 per cent at the core of the author's knowledge.

This may happen for all sorts of reasons. An author may feel that there is an abundance of books in their particular field and yet still feel they want to write something, so veer off the path by deciding to write a book about something different. I think this is a mistake. Write what you know, write what you are passionate about, starting with your why (thank you again Simon Sinek). I believe absolutely that you will find your own individual message that says something new and different, as long as you remain authentic and true to yourself.

Apart from anything else, it's much easier to write about what you know. As mentioned earlier, passion is like petrol in your tank. If you care deeply about your subject your writing will flow and you will find the task enjoyable as well as fulfilling.

Style and tone

Another question I get asked frequently is about the author's 'voice'. Sometimes first-time authors worry about this. It is easy to over-think it if you aren't used to writing.

My main advice to you is to be yourself first and foremost. You also need to think about who you are writing for, but if you try to ape a style that just isn't right for you your reader will feel your discomfort.

If you are working with a traditional publisher (see How should you publish?) make sure you have a really good understanding of what it is they are looking for and who their target market is. The more academic or theoretical style of book will require appropriate referencing systems, and possibly footnotes or other conventions. Whereas if you are writing a book that is more of a trade title, one that is likely to appeal to businesspeople rather than academics, you would not want to risk alienating your readers with academic conventions.

Business books range from the philosophical through to the 'how-to', practical and punchy. Think carefully about what will suit your purposes and those of your audience.

Should your book include illustrations?

Will the content of your book be easier to digest if you include visual material? Do you have models or diagrams that would help to explain your ideas well, or if not is this something you could be developing alongside your writing?

Or would the book benefit from other kinds of illustrations such as line drawings or photographs?

Sometimes authors come to me with ideas for books they feel would be enhanced with cartoons. This can work well, but again it is important to think about your audience first. If the content and your readers will be well served by you including cartoons, then go ahead, but make sure you aren't just adding things because there is a part of you that thinks the book is not 'enough'. Adding a dash of humour will not turn a deficient book into a good one.

How long should your book be?

The 'norm' on this has changed in recent years and will vary according to your audience. When I first started publishing I was reliably informed that a business book 'had to' contain a minimum of 60,000 words.

Now we are so used to gleaning high quality information in short bursts – there aren't many of us business owners who would actually find the time to read a book of that length. I think it's true to say that as long as the book does the job you need it to do, and that your readers need it to do, it simply does not matter how long it is.

Again, if working with a traditional publisher, check what is in your contract, or discuss it carefully with them before you sign. It's important that you deliver a book of the right length for their needs.

Type of book

How is your book going to be best presented? If you are publishing independently or self-publishing, the world is your oyster. Does it require lots of illustrations? Should it be in glorious full colour or is black and white text OK? Would a workbook style be best for your subject or your readers?

Should it be hardback (cased), with or without a dust jacket? Or is a paperback more appropriate for your readership? A hardback can look seriously impressive if that is important to you, and is not as expensive to do as you might think.

Or is your book going to be more suited to a Kindle-only version? If you are wanting to create information to get out to the world quickly and cheaply, then this might be a suitable route for you. You will, however, need to bear in mind it can be difficult to create enough visibility around a Kindle-only book.

Audio books are increasingly popular, turning the daily commute for thousands into an opportunity for learning and personal development. Audible, now owned by Amazon, delivers cost-effective audio books to phones and tablets via its subscription offerings or pay as you go. Previously popular with fiction publishers, more and more business publishers are creating audio versions of their current titles.

We are now seeing further possibilities for books combined with digital solutions. Recently my publishing company worked with Roger Harrop, the CEO expert, to publish his book, *Win! How to succeed in the new game of business*. He created a brilliant app to go with the book, and the book also contains a lot of QR codes that take the reader on an online journey as well as a simple reading experience. There is no doubt that digital developments are changing the book publishing landscape. Perhaps there is something that you could be doing that is a little new and different and will help your book (and therefore you) stand out from the crowd?

How to write your book

Once you've made the decision to write your book, you now need to make sure you have the resources and the support. Although this book is really about how to publish your business book, rather than how to write it, I am including a few tips to get you started. There are many very good books out there that will guide you if you want more help with writing – see resources on page 81.

Scheduling your writing time

Fail to plan, plan to fail as they say! Get writing time into your diary, and unless you work on your own it's probably a good idea to get away from the office, too. I know from personal experience how hard it is to focus on your writing in a busy office environment.

Make a date with yourself to deliver your manuscript in its first draft. If you are working to a publisher deadline, make sure this is several weeks after your date, giving yourself plenty of time to review your work. If you are publishing independently, decide when you want to publish your book and work back from there, making sure you have enough time in the diary to get the writing done.

If finding time in your regular calendar looks as if it will be an issue, think about booking a week or two away from it all on your own to write your book. I spent a glorious week in a quiet hotel in Majorca to break the back of this book, getting up early in the morning to write and then swimming in the afternoon. Bliss! If sunshine isn't for you, what about a cottage up the side of a mountain in Scotland or Wales? The main thing is just to get away from the normal routine of the office and focus on writing.

Work practice

Do your best to turn your emails off and your phone to silent while you are in writing mode, so that you can apply laser focus to it. There's nothing worse than losing your train of thought when you're on a roll because you got distracted by some irrelevant interruption.

Don't be a two-headed monster. When I write I'm aware that there are two heads that I could be using and I know I need to choose the appropriate one for the task. There is the creative head that allows the writing to flow. She is the one that comes up with the ideas and puts the words down one after the other. Without the creative head I wouldn't write at all. The second head is the editor head, which is rather different. She's a nit-picker, has a critical view and wants to organise and get every word correct. Without this head I would only ever write a bad book. Sometimes this head can attempt to bully the creative head – which frankly is not helpful for anyone. If the creative head is stopped in its tracks by the editor head there will not be a book to publish. Let the creative head do her job, tell the editor head to just kindly wait her turn and write freely. I think a lot of so-called writer's block is caused by two heads being involved.

It doesn't matter how you choose to allow these heads to work as long as they are separated. Some people may banish the editor head for a few days and bring her in to do her job after several thousand words have been written. Others may choose to end every writing session with a bit of time with the editor head on. Work out what is best for you and go with that.

Structure

I find it really helps me to start with the structure of the book. Not everyone works this way I appreciate, but for me a mind map really helps me to plan out my main themes and then add branches for the content. Other people may just prefer a simple outline with a list of chapter headings and then bullet points for your body content.

Whichever way you create your structure, don't ever feel you have to start at the top. In fact, I think it's often useful to write the introduction after you've written the book. Writing is a great way to discover how much you know! As Graham Jones so eloquently told me (see page 14) you will find you refine your thoughts as you write and you may surprise yourself as ideas turn up in your book that perhaps had previously only been half formed. Allow yourself the freedom to embrace this fully. It will enrich your work, your life and your business as well as your reader's experience.

Working with others – coach, editor, ghostwriter, co-authors

Publishing a book, as I hope this book has demonstrated, can be one of the most rewarding, satisfying and life-enhancing projects that any expert in their field can undertake. However, you are an expert at what you do and you may or may not enjoy the actual process of writing. A surprisingly high number of entrepreneurs are, in fact, dyslexic, which makes the act of writing particularly arduous.

Please, if for whatever reason, you are allowing yourself to be stopped from writing your book, know this. You don't have to do it all by yourself. So many people who aren't professional writers now want to write books for great reasons and have great books inside them; there is a plethora of help out there. Apart from the publishing professionals mentioned on pages 87–89, you might choose to work with a:

- book coach
- developmental editor (see page 87)
- ghostwriter
- co-author.

Time to commit

Make some notes now on what your book will be about and what it will be like. Include the following:

- What is your subject matter?
- What style and tone will you adopt?
- Will your book be theoretical, academic, or will it be more practical and problem solving?
- How long will your book be? How many pages, how many words?
- Will it include illustrations, and if so what type – diagrams, photos, line drawings and so on?

- Will your book be a workbook, a straight textbook, in full colour throughout or black and white?
- How will you write your book? In short bursts or will you take some time out to get it done?

Take out your diary and schedule time for writing in now. Start to think about the structure and how you will create it. Will you use a mind map or an outline list? Do you have everything you need to get started? Are you ready? Do you need help? If you think you do, what sort of help do you need?

“

Nuts!: Southwest Airline's crazy recipe for business and personal success by Kevin Freiberg (Texere Publishing, 2001)

This book inspired me because of the incredible personality of Herb Kelleher and how he built an awesome airline from nothing. It shares his strategies on customer service, sales, recruitment and how people with a common goal can achieve greatness.

Frank Furness
author of ***Walking with Tigers: Success secrets from the world's top business leaders*** *and* ***How to Find New Business and Clients***

”

How should you publish?

“

The Slight Edge: Turning simple differences into massive success and happiness by Jeff Olson (Gazelle, 2013)

The book is all about turning simple disciplines into massive success. In the book Jeff explains that just doing things won't make you successful. Doing the right things will make you successful and small steps every day over time create massive success.

Molly Harvey
Harvey Global
author of ***Outstanding Leadership***

”

How should you publish?

Choosing a publishing route for your book

If you have been tempted to write a book you are probably also familiar with a sense of uncertainty and confusion when it comes to thinking about how to get the thing published and out there into the world. These thoughts and feelings have been known to overwhelm the most robust of businesspeople, even those who don't usually let things stand in their way.

It's not really surprising. The publishing process can appear to be fraught with difficulty – where do you begin? Traditional publishers appear to put up barrier after barrier. You hear stories that you 'have to have an agent' or that they aren't open to any unsolicited submissions any more. I was once told with absolute certainty by the husband of one client I was working with that self-published books 'aren't worth the paper they're written on'.

But before you consign your manuscript to the bottom drawer of your desk, together with the blood, sweat and tears that have gone in to producing it, it would pay to take a more reasoned look at your options.

In Why publish a business book?, we looked at all the great reasons you might have to publish a book. Before you start on the search for a publishing option, it's a good idea to create a list of publishing objectives.

What do I want to achieve by writing and publishing this book?

If you didn't do this after reading Why publish a business book?, I suggest you do it now. Write down, in order of priority, what it is you want to achieve. If you are wanting to create authority so that you can build your business, how is it you are going to do that? If you are planning to find speaking opportunities, or build an online presence, how will the book support this?

I was once asked to set up a publishing imprint for an author who, apart from that one small task, was happy to self-publish. It was only after she had published her book that her book publicist rang and asked me how they could go about getting the book into airport shops, as this was a key part of their strategy for the author and her business. Naturally, they were fairly disappointed when I had to tell them that it was nigh impossible. Airport bookshop shelves are like Mayfair real estate, and without the substantial marketing budgets of the bigger publisher, it is highly unlikely a self-published book will gain a presence there.

How will this book change what I do?

Is your book a cornerstone for a new business, or is it going to help you diversify what you are doing already? If you are looking to get into new markets, will it be helpful to have freedom to do whatever you need with your book, or will it be more useful to have the opportunities afforded by partnership with a big publisher?

How will this book change the world?

Is the content of your book so groundbreaking that it will literally change the way lots of people think? Think about writers who have altered our thinking so much that we have even adopted phrases into everyday language – phrases such as Malcolm Gladwell's 'tipping point' or Andy Bounds' 'jelly effect'.

Who is the target audience? Who do I want to reach and influence?

After examining this in Who should you write for? you should now have a list of the type of people, any niche you want to appeal to and where in the world they are located. Knowing who you need to reach is a very important part of your strategy for deciding on a publishing route.

Academic writers might want to consider an academic publisher or a publisher of books erring towards the MBA reader – such as Kogan Page or perhaps the Pearson list, the Prentice Hall/ Financial Times Guides.

If you are wanting to appeal to small business owners, imprints such as the Wiley lists, of which Capstone is one, or this book's imprint, the Authority Guides, might be more appropriate.

If your main aim is to use your book as a calling card, you will want to weigh up whether your needs marry with a traditional publisher's. Also the cost to buy your books from a publisher will be considerably higher than paying for a print run of an independently published book.

How will I get the book into the world? How will I sell the book?

Again, it's important to think this through before deciding on a publishing route. If your plan is absolutely dependent on getting your book into airport shops, you will need to be clear about that right from the start and pick your publisher carefully. Not all publishers, even of a traditional type, will be able to guarantee the very high exposure of your book. It will depend enormously on their marketing budget at the time and how commercial your book is in reality likely to be.

The business end of publishing

It may help to take some time to think about publishing business models and how each one works from a financial perspective.

Fifty years ago, there was really only one way that you could go about publishing a book and that was to work with what tends nowadays to be termed a 'traditional publishing house'.

Traditional publishing

A traditional publishing house is a business that makes its profit from the sales of books as physical and digital products in its own domestic and also (usually) foreign markets. It will also make money from the licensing of those products to other publishers or other companies through translation rights sales, or other subsidiary rights such as large print formats or audio.

As an author you are a supplier to this company. It is important to note this. I find quite frequently that authors believe their relationship to the publisher is as a customer. This is simply not the case. The publisher has to create a product to sell and it does so by using the skills and talents of many people: designers, editors, typesetters, illustrators, printers. And authors are, in one sense, simply a part of that process.

The second, essential job for a publisher is to distribute their books as widely as possible. They will do this through the book trade using wholesalers such as Gardners and Bertrams to reach the retailers such as Amazon, Waterstones, WHSmith and so on, plus any other outlets that may be open to them. The larger houses may also deal directly with the retailers. Without the successful marketing and promotion of your book, a publisher doesn't stand much chance of selling it – and if they don't sell their books they don't make their profits, simple as that.

From the point of view of an author as a supplier, there is no actual cost to working with a publisher – beyond the blood, sweat and tears of the actual writing of course! An author may be asked to cough up for what are sometimes seen as 'extras', such as permissions work (getting the agreement of people you quote extensively in your work) or indexing.

At the end of the process, once the book is published, you should receive a share of the profits from the sales – which will normally be around 8–10 per cent of net income. This is likely to equate to around 4–5 per cent of the cover price after taking into consideration the trade discounts required by wholesalers and retailers. Some publishers will pay part of this in the form of an 'advance' after you have signed a contract with them agreeing to their terms. This advance is often split into two payments: 50 per cent on the signing of the contract and the balance on receipt of an acceptable manuscript.

To find out more about approaching a traditional publisher with your idea see page 55.

Author-funded, independent publishing

Another option is to seek the services of a publishing company that adopts a different business model. In this set-up you would receive all the professional services of a publisher, but you would pay for them.

How much you pay will generally depend on the level of professionalism involved. Low-cost packages are available if you are on a tight budget, but you will need to be aware that the production of a high-quality book that is well designed, carefully edited and proofread, and printed to a high standard is never going to be cheap. If you want to give a good impression of yourself, you should find a budget of around £5,000–10,000 to be sure you are creating something of value that will make you proud and draw the right kind of attention.

Working with this kind of publisher, you would normally retain full publishing rights and ownership of all the content and you can purchase books to suit your requirements.

A publisher such as this should also be able to offer you full distribution services so that your book is available to bookstores as well as on Amazon. The bulk of the profits from net sales of books are returned to the author, although there may be additional costs for the distribution of your book. Expect to receive around 25–30 per cent of the full cover price after any costs.

Self-publishing

In the same way as musicians have in recent years begun to create and publish their own music, so authors have taken the job of publishing their work into their own hands.

With the rise of print-on-demand suppliers such as Lightning Source, Lulu and Amazon's CreateSpace, as well as digital platforms such as Kindle and Apple's iTunes, it has become easier than ever before for authors to hoe their own row and do away with the professional services or distribution networks of the traditional publisher.

As sole owner of the publishing project the author also has to finance it. As with working with an independent publisher, you will need to put the appropriate budget together. Later on in this chapter, we will look at what you will need to do to create your book; however, once again it is important to understand that using the professional services of freelancers who are experienced in book production may not be the cheapest way to do it, but it will definitely deliver better results.

After paying any commissions to the distribution platforms available to them, the author retains all the profits. There are limitations to be aware of here that we will look at later, but essentially sales of a self-published book through Amazon will return around 40 per cent of the cover price of physical books and around 70 per cent without VAT (for ebooks between $9.99 and $2.99) or 35 per cent without VAT (for ebooks over $9.99) of the price of an ebook.

Having looked at the business end of the various publishing routes, it's now time to dig a little deeper and explore the way each route works in more detail so that you can make an informed choice about which is the best way for you to choose.

Should you choose a traditional publisher for your book?

First of all, it has to be said that not every book is suitable for a traditional publishing route. This doesn't mean it has any less value or that somehow it will be seen as inferior. At the end of the day, a book will be judged on its merits and not on its publisher, although some authors may believe that the brand of a big publisher has helped them look more credible.

To have your idea accepted, your book will need to be 100 per cent commercially viable. Book publishers are essentially product manufacturers and, as we have seen earlier in this chapter, they need to sell books in order to regain their outgoing costs of production, cover all their overheads and make money for their shareholders.

Today, the book industry is an increasingly difficult one to make money in. According to the Booksellers Association, in 2005 there were 1,535 bookshops in the UK. By 2015 this number had dropped to 894. Margins have been squeezed so that the returns on actual sales of books have dropped considerably as the discounting of books has become ubiquitous.

In fact, most of us as customers probably appreciate the fact that we can now go online, find a book that will help us with whatever issue we are facing, order it and either read it immediately if we buy a digital copy or receive it the very next day if we want a physical one. And we probably like the fact that the book is very low cost, as well as the fact that we haven't had to move away from our desk or our armchair.

For a publisher, this means selling more and more books. It is hardly surprising therefore that they have become increasingly risk averse. They will only ever consider publishing a book when they can clearly identify a healthy target market for it.

Most publishers therefore will want to see three things:

- First, a good, original idea. While ideas are rarely completely new, a publisher likes to see a fresh approach to a familiar subject. They are also likely to be looking for new books in fields that are hot right now. Does your book cover a subject that lots of people are talking about currently? How will it be potentially world changing (without being too radical and risky to publish)?

- Second, ask yourself, are you the right person to write this book? You need to have a broad network and you should be a proficient public speaker – the more speaking you do the better. Ideally you should already have a good PR message and representation. While you may not have celebrity status (yet), it's a good idea to adopt the mindset of being willing to take centre stage. You will need to convince a publisher that you have a strong following of people who will willingly buy your book. The reason that publishers love celebrities is because their admirers buy the books!
- Third, know if books like yours sell well. This is the hardest one to judge as an industry outsider, but check out books like yours on Amazon and see how many make bestseller status.

Which publishers should you approach?

There are a number of ways to put together a list of publishers you might want to approach.

First of all it's a good idea to create a shortlist of publishers – you can do this by checking out the hugely useful resource for authors, the *Writers and Artists Yearbook*, which lists all the publishers and agents in the UK and Ireland. This book comes out every year in August, and is also available via a (paid) subscription online at www.writersandartists.co.uk/listings, where you can use the search facility to find the appropriate publisher for your book.

Table 1 Compilation of business publishers

Publisher	Imprint	Description	Recent publications
Bloomsbury	Bloomsbury Information Ltd	'Bloomsbury's Business and Management books offer unique and invaluable insights into all aspects of the business world, from leadership and coaching to innovation and analytical thinking.' Their topics include – general business and management, careers and self improvement, corporate and social responsibility, finance and economics, HR and training, international perspectives, leadership and coaching, marketing, small business, startups and entrepreneurship and strategy.	Fiona Elsa Dent and Viki Holton, *How to Thrive and Survive as a Working Woman: The coach-yourself toolkit* (Apr 2016) Ian Goldin and Chris Kutarna, *Age of Discovery: Navigating the risks and rewards of our new Renaissance* (May 2016)
Crimson Publishing	Crimson	Crimson Publishing specialises in niche magazines and online publishing. They provide 'practical and inspiring information for people looking to start or grow businesses.'	Jo Haigh, *The Keys to the Boardroom: How to get there and how to stay there* (Jan 2014) Annie Ashdown, *The Confidence Factor: The seven secrets of successful people* (Sep 2013)

Edward Elgar	Edward Elgar Publishing Ltc	Academic and professional publisher. Their business research topics include entrepreneurship, leadership, organisation studies, human resource management, marketing and strategy. Visit this page for guidelines and advice on submitting a proposal: www.e-elgar.com/submitting-proposal	Arnis Sauka, Friedrich Schneider and Colin C. Williams, *Entrepreneurship and the Shadow Economy* (May 2016) Suze Wilson, *Thinking Differently about Leadership: A critical history of leadership studies* (May 2016)
Hachette UK	Center Street	Center Street publishes non-fiction books in categories such as political, leadership, sports, health and fitness, autobiography and current events.	John C. Maxwell, *What Successful People Know About Leadership: Advice from America's #1 leadership Authority* (May 2016) Rich DeVos, *Ten Powerful Phrases for Positive People* (Jan 2016)

Publisher	Imprint	Description	Recent publications
Hachette UK	John Murray Press	An 'unashamedly populist' imprint, publishing fiction, non-fiction, gift and humour books.	Matthew Syed, *Black Box Thinking: Marginal gains and the secrets of high performance* (Apr 2016) Laszlo Bock, *Work Rules!: Insights from inside Google that will transform how you live and lead* (Mar 2016)
	Nicholas Brealey	Nicholas Brealey specialises in 'notable books', with topics such as coaching and leadership, personal development, and business and economics.	Jocelyn Davis, *The Greats on Leadership: Classic wisdom for modern managers* (May 2016)
HarperCollins	Harper Business	'The gold standard in business book publishing for more than half a century' Harper Business publishes books on business, management and economics.	Thomas Davenport, *Only Humans Need Apply: Winners and losers in the age of smart machines* (Jun 2016) Henry Cloud, *The Power of the Other: The startling effect other people have on you, from the boardroom to the bedroom and beyond – and what to do about it* (Jun 2016)

Kogan Page	Kogan Page	Publisher of specialist professional books. Topics include business, risk and information management, marketing and public relations, HR, organisational development and coaching, logistics, operations and supply chain management, employability and careers and entrepreneurship. Information on publishing with Kogan Page: www.koganpage.com/page/publish-a-book Guidelines on creating a book proposal are provided in a document that can be found at the bottom of the page.	Brian MacNeice and James Bowen, *Powerhouse: Insider accounts into the world's top high-performance organizations* (Oct 2016) Claire Brooks, *Marketing with Strategic Empathy: Inspiring strategy with deeper consumer insight* (Aug 2016)
Legend Times Ltd	Legend Business	Launched in 2010, Legend Business plans to build 'a wide-ranging, interactive and dynamic list of business titles.'	David Bateman, *Business Plans that Get Investment* (Apr 2016) Jonathan Reuvid, *Investors' Guide to the United Kingdom 2015/16* (Oct 2015)

Publisher	Imprint	Description	Recent publications
Management Books 2000	Management Books 2000	Management Books 2000 publish 'working books for working managers', with topics including business development, management skills, finance, HR, sales and marketing.	Steven Harris, *Fired Up and Ready to Go!: Developing life-changing skills to benefit you and your customer* (Sep 2015) Alasdair Drysdale, *The Interim Director: 40 projects in the wilderness … and a lot of sound advice* (Nov 2014)
McGraw-Hill Education	McGraw-Hill Education	Publishes general educational books, including a wide range of business and management books.	Bill Capodagli and Lynn Jackson, *The Disney Way: Harnessing the management secrets of Disney in your company*, 3rd edn. (May 2016) Marie Perruchet, *One Perfect Pitch: How to sell your Idea, your product, your business – or yourself* (Apr 2016)

Oneworld Publications	Oneworld	Oneworld focuses on non-fiction, including general business books. Guidelines for book proposals: https://oneworld-publications.com/book-proposals	William Poundstone, *Head in the Cloud: The power of knowledge in the age of Google* (Sep 2016) Therese Huston, *How Women Decide: What's true, what's not, and why it matters* (Jul 2016)
Pearson	Pearson Business	A leading publisher in business and personal development. Guidelines for book proposals: http://bit.ly/2cwOZks	Richard Newton, *Project Management Step by Step: How to plan and manage a highly successful project* (Jul 2016)
	Financial Times Publishing	A collaboration between the *Financial Times* and Pearson, FT Publishing publishes books in the areas of general business, finance and investing, sales and marketing, leadership, management and strategy, human resources, and global business. Guidelines for book proposals: http://bit.ly/2cXNAEX	Pam Jones, Angela Jowitt and Viki Holton, *How to Coach Your Team: Release team potential and hit peak performance* (Aug 2016) Owen Walker, *Barbarians in the Boardroom: Activist investors and the battle for control of the world's most powerful companies* (May 2016)

Publisher	Imprint	Description	Recent publications
Penguin	Ebury Press	A leading publisher of non-fiction books, they have also developed a reputation for highly commercial fiction.	Antonio García Martínez, *Chaos Monkeys: Inside the Silicon Valley money machine* (Jun 2016)
	Portfolio	Launched in 2010, Portfolio publishes personal development and business books. 'Whether it's leadership, personal development, entrepreneurship, finance or innovation, Portfolio publishes the cutting edge of business thinking with attitude and impact.'	David Butler, Linda Tischler, *Design to Grow: How Coca-Cola learned to combine scale and agility (and how you can, too)* (Feb 2016) James Watt, *Business for Punks: Break all the rules – the BrewDog way* (Feb 2016)
	Random House Business Books	Includes well-known and respected books on leadership and management, economics, and business skills.	Hayagreeva Rao and Robert I. Sutton, *Scaling up Excellence: Getting to more without settling for less* (Aug 2016) Chris Voss and Tahl Raz, *Never Split the Difference: Negotiating as if your life depended on it* (May 2016)

Penguin	Virgin Books	Virgin Books publishes a broad range of non-fiction books.	Brian Wong, *The Cheat Code: The secret tweaks, hacks and tips to get noticed and get ahead* (Sept 2016) Estanislao Bachrach, *The Agile Mind: How your brain makes creativity happen* (May 2016)
	WH Allen	An imprint of Ebury Press. WH Allen publishes 'provocative and intelligent conversation-starters for the modern world.' This includes politics, popular science, history and current affairs titles.	Adam Grant, *Originals: How Non-conformists change the world* (Feb 2016)
Profile Books	Profile Books	Publishers of 'stimulating non-fiction in a wide range of fields, including history, business and economics, science and biography, with a sprinkling of humour.' They publish books in partnership with the Chartered Management Institute and *The Economist*.	Sue Unerman and Kathryn Jacob, *The Glass Wall: Success strategies for women at work – and businesses that mean business* (Sep 2016) Ryan Holiday, *Ego is the Enemy: The fight to master our greatest opponent* (Jul 2016)

Publisher	Imprint	Description	Recent publications
Routledge	Routledge	Leading academic publisher. Their business-related topics include HR management, international business, leadership, strategic management and more.	Jim O'Hare, *Analysing Financial Statements for Non-Specialists* 2nd edn. (Oct 2016) Angela Dunbar, *Clean Coaching: The insider guide to making change happen* (Oct 2016)
Simon & Schuster UK	Economist Books	Imprint for *The Economist*, includes a 'The Economist Guide' series among other titles.	Anna Faelten, Michael Driessen and Scott Moeller, *Why Deals Fail and How to Rescue Them: M&A lessons for business success* (Sep 2016) Navi Radjou and Jaideep Prabhu, *Frugal Innovation: How to do better with less* (Aug 2016)

Simon & Schuster UK	Gallery Books	'We are dedicated to publishing a wide variety of must-read books on a wide array of interesting topics. It is an imprint designed to showcase established voices and to introduce emerging new ones – in both fiction and nonfiction, and across a variety of genres.'	Erik Bertrand Larssen, *Hell Week: Seven days to be your best self* (Jun 2016) Brent D. Peterson and Gaylan W. Nielson, *Fake Work: Why people are working harder than ever but accomplishing less, and how to fix the problem* (Oct 2014)
	Simon & Schuster	The Simon & Schuster imprint is a 'cornerstone of the company and one of the most venerated brand names in the world of publishing'. Amongst other non-fiction, they publish various business and economics books.	Ric Edelman, *Rescue Your Money: How to invest your money during these tumultuous times* (Jul 2016) Jonah Berger, *Invisible Influence: The hidden forces that shape behavior* (Jun 2016)
	Touchstone	The smallest 'boutique imprint' at Simon & Schuster, Touchstone's non-fiction publications include some business-related self-help and advice books.	Rachel S. Moore, *The Artist's Compass: The complete guide to building a life and a living in the performing arts* (May 2016) David Schwartz, *The Magic of Thinking Big* (Oct 2015)

Publisher	Imprint	Description	Recent publications
Wiley	Capstone	Capstone publishes business and personal development books, written by authors who are experts in their fields.	Paul McGee, *How to Speak so People Really Listen: The straight-talking guide to communicating with influence and impact* (Oct 2016) Pat Divilly, *Upgrade Your Life: How to take back control and achieve your goals* (Oct 2016)
	For Dummies	The well-known Dummies series of reference books offers information on various topics that may appear difficult or intimidating at first.	Neil Cobb and Charlie Divine, *Writing Business Bids and Proposals For Dummies* (Aug 2016) Eric Tyson, *Investing For Dummies*, 7th edn. (Jun 2016)

Make sure you understand the lists of books that publishers own, and identify those for which your book may be a good fit. Check out your own bookshelves and identify the publishers of books like the one you are proposing to write.

The first thing to do once you've identified a suitable publisher is to go to their website and download a copy of their author guidelines.

Writing a proposal

It pays before you start to write your proposal to think as commercially as you can from the publisher's point of view. Why should they want to publish your book above all others? Stand in their shoes for a bit. Look at your project as objectively as you can and examine with a cool mind whether there really is a business case for publishing it, not from your standpoint, but from theirs.

Take a good look at the guidelines provided by the publisher you are pitching to. Having looked carefully at them, are you still sure they are the right publisher for you? If so, make sure you mark out several hours in which to prepare your pitch, sticking closely to the guidelines. Don't be tempted to leave anything out. Commissioning editors receive dozens of enquiries every week and won't give your proposal a second look if you don't present it in the way they want to see it.

Don't make the mistake of writing the whole book before you pitch to a publisher. They will probably want to feel they will have some input into your book and it can concern a commissioning editor if they feel you have already completed the manuscript. Even if you have written your book, it may be wise to simply submit one chapter and a list of contents, and keep an open mind about changing your content to suit your editor.

Perhaps the most important thing to bear in mind when you are writing your proposal is this: publishers are aware that healthy book sales are much more likely when they are generated by the author themselves. The full engagement and commitment of the author is what makes a book fly when it comes to marketing. You may have a great idea, but if you expect the publisher to be solely responsible for marketing and selling the book you will be unlikely to convince them to take you on.

Take a look at the Wiley guidelines for new authors: http://media.wiley.com/assets/2256/92/wiley_capstone_new_book_proposal.pdf

You will see that there is one page of questions about the book, and two pages about your profile and your marketing plan. That is a big indication of the priorities of one of the biggest business book publishers. You will need to show them that you have a wide network of contacts, that you are a good public speaker, and that you are willing and able to get out there and promote your book. In other words, if you want a book contract you will need to prove that you are no shrinking violet. Be careful though. There is a balance to be drawn between being seen as overly arrogant and a position of confidence and authority.

Here are some of the ways that you can provide evidence of a profile that a publisher will find attractive:

- Your recent past and planned forthcoming speaking schedule
- The number of followers in your social media networks
- Your membership of professional organisations
- Any awards, medals, prizes you have won for your achievements in business
- Access to other authorities (particularly any big names who may endorse you and your book)

- Any relevant press coverage you have received
- Articles you've written or that have been written about you or your business
- A regularly written blog with evidence of a healthy readership

The publishing contract

The publishing contract or author agreement passes to the publisher the exclusive rights to publish your book. This agreement prevents you or anyone else from replicating the content of your book elsewhere, so this is another reason for you to think carefully about whether this is the right route for you. For instance, if you have plans to use the content of your book in other ways, it will be important to check this carefully with the publisher and perhaps also with a specialist lawyer before signing anything. You do not want to find that by publishing a book you actually put obstacles in the way of the healthy progress of your business plan. If you find this is the case, carefully consider publishing independently so that you can retain full control over your intellectual property (see page 72).

In the agreement you make, you will also effectively be allowing a publisher to seek to sell the rights to your book on to another publisher (usually one in a different country). Your book may therefore be published in a number of different countries, for which you will be paid an agreed royalty.

The contract will include the following elements:

- The date by which you will promise to deliver the manuscript
- The length (in words) that you have agreed your manuscript should be
- The agreed royalty rate for sales of books in the home territory, both physical and digital (which will probably differ)

- The agreed royalty rate for sales of foreign rights and book sales in other territories
- The number of complimentary copies you as author will be given
- A possible 'option' clause requesting the right to first refusal on your next book or books

Some publishers are also now including a 'buy-back' clause in their contracts, when an author is required to buy a certain number of copies of their own book at a discounted price. Make sure you do your sums carefully before agreeing to such a clause. I have seen contracts where the publisher requires the author to buy 6,000 copies over three years. You could be committing to a very large liability indeed, if for some reason you are unable to secure these kind of sales.

Once you have found a publisher willing to take your book on, it's a good idea to get a professional to look over the contract. This could be a specialist lawyer, an author's agent or you can join the Society of Authors (http://www.societyofauthors.org/) who will scrutinise the details for you and give you advice.

Choosing to publish independently

While it is true to say that getting your book commissioned by a publishing house may be possible and the right route for some, many people publishing a book to help them grow their business will end up choosing a more independent approach.

There are many things to be said for staying independent of a traditional publishing contract. You will be able to do what you like with the content of your book or books since you have not parted with the right to publish it. You are therefore free to repurpose and exploit your material in any way that you choose, which could be a problem if you are in partnership with a traditional publisher. You will own the physical books themselves, as well as the files of the digital versions. You won't have to buy copies of your books from the publisher – you can print your own books or buy them at a low price from your independent publishing company.

Taking the list of your priorities that you created in Why publish a business book?, examine again your business reasons for publishing a book. Look too at the list of people you want to get your book in front of and your considered plan for how to reach them (Who should you write for?). You should by now have a clear picture in your mind of your objectives and of how you're going to maximise the potential for your book. Your choice of independent route will depend very much on how strong the business case is for your book. We will look closely at two independent routes to publication that you could choose from.

Self-publishing

Here I want to draw a clear distinction between the two independent routes. There are many publishers who call themselves 'self-publishing houses' these days, and to my mind this is somewhat confusing. In my terminology, self-publishing applies to those authors who literally do their own publishing work. They may not necessarily do every job, but the author will probably project manage the production of the book. A so-called 'self-publishing house' would be better named an author-funded, independent publisher. See page 54 for more details about the difference in this sort of company's business model.

If you choose a true self-publishing route, it means putting together your own team. Below you will find a list of the minimum recommended professional team members:

- Copy editor
- Graphic designer

- Typesetter/layout artist
- Ebook creator
- Proofreader

Depending on your project, some other services you may need to consider using are:

- Developmental editor
- Photographer
- Illustrator
- Indexer
- Permissions editor
- Legal advisor
- Rights specialist

Self-publishers can apply to the ISBN Agency for an imprint (your publishing brand name) and a list of numbers – International Standard Book Numbers (ISBNs) – and submit the details of the first title to the Agency. ISBNs are bought in sets of 10 or 100 and you need a unique ISBN for each version of your book – print, ebook and so on. You can find the relevant forms and information at the link in the resources section of this book.

By registering your book or books in this way you effectively become a publisher of your own book – hence you are self-published. This part of the process is done in the same way as a publisher does it – the only difference being that a publisher has access to enhanced listings that give books more visibility online and in traditional book trade catalogues.

Today you can self-publish in a simple, although slightly more limited way through a print-on-demand (POD) route. One method of doing this is through Amazon. You don't even need to register your imprint, as Amazon will apply an ISBN for you.

You can upload your book using the Amazon tools and it will be available on Kindle almost immediately. You can also provide a book cover and load the book into CreateSpace so that Amazon can supply you with printed copies of your book, too – although you don't have to order large quantities. In fact, you are free to order none, one or hundreds; it's entirely up to you.

This is a very low budget way of publishing your book. However, the availability of your book is limited to Amazon and you will have to compete with thousands of other books on the same platform using the same tools: because it is so low cost it is extremely popular. So you will need to be realistic about whether this route will create the exposure you need and want for your book. Also, if you do need a large quantity of books, POD can get rather expensive. So make sure you do your sums and create a realistic plan before you pick your independent publishing route. A more professional service may pay you dividends in the long run.

Author-funded independent publishing

If your objective is to grow your business by creating a profile and establishing yourself as an authority in your field, you may find that stepping away from working on your business in order to project manage the self-publishing of a book ends up being nothing more than a costly distraction. A professional publishing services company could be the solution.

Finding a company to work with is similar to choosing any professional services firm. You will want to do careful research to make sure you find the right people to work with that will suit you and your book project. Here's a suggested checklist of things to consider:

- Quality of book products they create (ask them for samples).
- Do you like the cover designs they have produced previously?

- Are they happy to work flexibly with you to make sure you get the product you want?
- Will they advise you and make sure you don't publish a book that isn't as good as it could be?
- How do you find their customer service? Are they friendly and helpful when you call or email?
- Do they distribute through the book trade or will your book only be available on Amazon?
- Is the offering POD only? If so, are you happy with the options offered and is the cost of printing reasonable?
- Do they offer extra marketing support, such as PR or social media campaigns, should you need it?

However you choose to publish, the independent publishing route may be a challenge for any author, but it is a challenge that can be hugely rewarding. When you undo the parcel containing a book with your name on the cover, you will be able to say 'I did that' and feel, quite rightly, very proud indeed.

Time to commit

Taking account of your list of objectives, weigh up which route will work best for you by making a list of pros and cons for:

- Approaching a traditional publisher
- Self-publishing
- Working with an author-funded independent publisher

You may consider engaging a publishing consultant or coach to help you with this process.

Begin your publishing journey

The Chimp Paradox: The mind management programme to help you achieve success, confidence and happiness by Prof Steve Peters (Vermilion, 2012)

Excellent communication is imperative in both our personal and professional relationships. I found that this book helped to explain why and how we respond in different situations. This can be especially useful when it comes to negotiating. Understanding how someone else is either responding to you emotionally or logically is an invaluable tool. This book has helped me to bring the best out in myself, and also others.

Elaine Hanzak
speaker
*author of **Eyes without Sparkle: A journey through postnatal illness** and **Another Twinkle in the Eye: Contemplating another pregnancy after perinatal mental illness***

Begin your publishing journey

In this book we have looked together at *why* you should consider publishing a business book, *who* you should write your book for, *what* your book should be, *how* you should write it and, finally, *how* you should publish.

If you have made some notes as suggested in the 'Time to commit' sections at the end of each chapter, you will have the bones of a good publishing plan. There should be nothing to stop you now.

If you are indeed convinced you need to get published but you need some help, please don't hesitate to visit our blog at the SRA Books website (suerichardson.co.uk), where the SRA team offer tips, encouragement, inspiration and information to help you on your way to becoming a published author.

I look forward to seeing your book in print.

> Until one is committed, there is hesitancy, the chance to draw back – concerning all acts of initiative (and creation), there is one elementary truth that ignorance of which kills countless ideas and splendid plans: that the moment one definitely commits oneself, then Providence moves too. All sorts of things occur to help one that would never otherwise have occurred. A whole stream of events issues from the decision, raising in one's favour all manner

of unforeseen incidents and meetings and material assistance, which no man could have dreamed would have come his way.

Whatever you can do, or dream you can do, begin it. Boldness has genius, power, and magic in it. Begin it now.

W H Murray

Resources

Reading list

Baverstock, A. (2011) *The Naked Author: A guide to self-publishing*. London: Bloomsbury.

Carnegie, D. (2006) *How to Win Friends and Influence People*. Vermilion.

Cialdini, R. (2008) *Influence: Science and practice*. Pearson.

Cooke, C. (2009) *PR Demystified: How to get free publicity by giving journalists what they really need.* The HotHive

Cooke, C. (2016) *The Authority Guide to Marketing your Business Book: 52 easy-to-follow tips from a book PR expert*. Authority Guides.

Craven, R. (2011) *Grow your Service Firm: How to run a successful service-based business.* Crimson Publishing.

Craven, R. (2015) *Grow your Digital Agency.* CreateSpace Independent Publishing Platform.

Frankl, V. E. (2004) *Man's Search for Meaning: The classic tribute to hope from the Holocaust*. Rider.

Freiberg, K. (2001) *Nuts!: Southwest Airline's crazy recipe for business and personal success*. Texere Publishing.

Gerber, M. (1995) *The E-Myth Revisited: Why most small businesses don't work and what to do about it*. New York: HarperCollins.

Godin, S. (2005) *Purple Cow: Transform your business by being remarkable*. London: Penguin.

Godin, S. (2008) *Tribes: We need you to lead us*. Piatkus.

Grayson, J. (2016) *Landscapes of the Heart: The working world of a sex and relationship therapist*. Jessica Kingsley Publishers.

Harrop, R. (2014) *Win! How to succeed in the new game of business*. SRA Books.

Henson, J. (2014) *What's Your Excuse For Not Eating Healthily? Set aside your excuses and improve your relationship with food*. CompletelyNovel.

Henson, J. (2013) *What's Your Excuse For Not Getting Fit? Overcome your excuses and get active, healthy and happy*. CompletelyNovel.

Jefferson, S. and Tanton, S. (2015) *Valuable Content Marketing: How to make quality content your key to success*. London: Kogan Page.

Johnson, T. (2016) *The Success Book: How to grow yourself and your business*. LID Publishing.

Jones, G. (2014) *Clickology: What works in online shopping and how your business can use consumer psychology to succeed*. Nicholas Brealey.

Jones, G. (2015) *Sales Genius: 40 insights from the science of selling*. John Murray Learning.

Kotter, J. (2008) *A Sense of Urgency*. Harvard Business Press.

Kotter, J. and Rathgeber, H. (2006) *Our Iceberg is Melting: Changing and succeeding under any conditions*. St. Martin's Press.

Lopata, A. (2011) *Recommended: How to sell through networking and referrals*. Harlow: Pearson.

Lopata, A. (2011) *...and Death Came Third! The definitive guide to networking and speaking in public*. 2nd edn. Ecademy Press.

Maister, D. (2003) *Managing the Professional Service Firm*. New edn. Simon & Schuster UK.

Maltz, M. (2003) *The New Psycho-Cybernetics: The original science of self-improvement and success that has changed the lives of 30 million people*. Prentice Hall Press.

McGee, P. (2015) *S.U.M.O. (Shut Up, Move On): The straight-talking guide to succeeding in life*. 10th Anniversary edn. Capstone.

Murray, W. (1951) *The Scottish Himalayan Expedition*. J.M. Dent & Sons.

Olson, J. (2013) *The Slight Edge: Turning simple differences into massive success and happiness*. Gazelle.

Peters, S. (2012) *The Chimp Paradox: The mind management programme to help you achieve success, confidence and happiness*. Vermilion.

Purkiss, J. and Royston-Smith, D. (2012) *Brand You: Turn your unique talents into a winning formula.* 2nd edn. Pearson.

Rand, A. (2007) *Atlas Shrugged*. Updated edn. Penguin Classics.

Reynard, J. (2016) *The Spiritual Route to Entrepreneurial Success: From harassed sole trader to visionary CEO.* AuthorHouseUK.

Sinek, S. (2011) *Start with Why: How great leaders inspire everyone to take action*. Penguin.

Stevens, A. and du Toit, P. (2013) *The Exceptional Speaker: How to deliver sensational speeches.* Congruence Press.

Stevens, A. (2010) *Ping: How to tap into the power of traditional and social media to massively improve your profile and profits.* Lean Marketing Press.

Stevens, A. and Nicholas, J. (2009) *MediaMasters: Insider secrets from the big names of broadcast, print and social media.* Bookshaker.

Taylor, W. and LaBarre, P. (2011) *Mavericks at Work: Why the most original minds in business win*. Harper.

Thomas, B. (2013) *Watertight Marketing: Delivering long-term sales results*. St Albans: Anoma Press.

Trout, J. (2008) *Differentiate or Die: Survival in our era of killer competition*. John Wiley & Sons.

Walters, L. (1993) *Secrets of Successful Speakers: How you can motivate, captivate and persuade*. McGraw-Hill Education.

Weiss, A. (2016) *Million Dollar Consulting: The professional's guide to growing a practice*. 5th edn. McGraw-Hill Education.

Winter, B. (2009) *Making a Living without a Job: Winning ways for creating work that you love*. Revised edn. Bantam Books Inc.

Wusche, V. (2016) *Using Other People's Money: How to invest in property.* 4th edn. SRA Books.

Wusche, V. (2012) *Make More Money from Property: From investor thinking to a business mindset.* SRA Books.

Wusche, V. (2012) *Property for the Next Generation: Preparing your family for a wealthy future.* SRA Books.

List of organisations and other resources

Society of Authors http://www.societyofauthors.org/

Society for Editors and Proofreaders http://www.sfep.org.uk/

Writers and Artists Yearbook
https://www.writersandartists.co.uk/

ISBN Agency
http://www.isbn.nielsenbook.co.uk/controller.php?page=123

Nielsen Book Data http://www.nielsenbookdata.co.uk/

Alliance of Independent Authors
https://www.allianceindependentauthors.org/

Atlas Shrugged by Ayn Rand (Penguin Classics, updated edn, 2007)

My favourite book of all time is *Atlas Shrugged* by Ayn Rand. It's a massive book: 1072 pages in nine point font. I've read it nine times and given away about 300 copies of it to family, friends and clients. I'm guessing very few of them have read it. However, those who have always report it was life changing. Ayn Rand promulgates the philosophy of objectivism and *Atlas Shrugged* is a brilliantly crafted novel about the struggle of entrepreneurs in an increasingly bureaucratic world. The heroine Dagny Taggert is an inspiration to anyone, especially with her line: 'I decided I would place nothing, nothing above the verdict of my own mind.'

Peter Thomson
author of ***The Secrets of Communication: Be heard and get results***

Appendix: Who's in a professional publishing team?

A developmental or structural editor

This is a person who will help you if you are not a born writer and who knows about creating a book that works. They will help you with the structure of the book and make sure that it flows, accurately delivers the information required and makes perfect sense to the reader.

A book designer

It's important to find someone who understands about publishing books. There are particular technical skills required in preparing a book for print, as well as the need to understand what makes a cover work for a particular target audience. You need someone who has experience of all of this to guide you in making the right decisions.

A copy editor

The next stage in the editing process is copy-editing – sometimes known as line editing. It's the copy editor's job to get the punctuation, grammar and spelling knocked into shape, and also to pick up on anything that isn't completely clear to them and therefore will be unlikely to be understood by the reader. They will be less intrusive than a developmental editor and will probably list queries for you, rather than rewrite, unless you give them permission to do so. It's important to brief your copy editor carefully so you are on the right wavelength from the start.

A typesetter

Plonking a load of words into Word or some other word processing package will not make a pretty book! The industry standard software used by today's typesetters is InDesign, although a few are still using QuarkXPress. Make sure you use a typesetter who is experienced in book publishing and preferably can create your ebook files as well, to save you paying someone twice for the job.

A proofreader

Many people wonder why we use both a copy editor and a proofreader – isn't it the same job? they ask. Well, the answer is yes and no. It's entirely up to you whether you use both, but if you do only use one I suggest you use a copy editor. It is much cheaper to make extensive changes in a manuscript than it is to do it at proof stage, after typesetting. However, we would always add a professional proofreader into our project team. You'd be surprised how much can get missed along the way and a fresh pair of eyes at the final stage before print will always pick up minor errors that may have crept in during the typesetting process.

Generally a proofreader will be even less intrusive than a copy editor – although the two terms may be used almost interchangeably these days – so check with your proofreader and, again, give them a good brief before they start work so you know what it is you are asking of them.

Professional editors and proofreaders can be found through the Society for Editors and Proofreaders, www.sfep.org.uk

A printer

Some people make the mistake of using their local printer to print their books. Do be sure that you've seen samples of books they have printed, not just their brochures, business cards, flyers and so on. Again there are technical differences with books that can lead to problems if the printer doesn't have relevant experience.

A publisher

If you self-publish this means you! The job still needs to be done though. This means applying for ISBNs, registering the book properly, complying with the Copyright Law and many other things. For all the details of this, I strongly recommend reading a book by Alison Baverstock, *The Naked Author: A guide to self-publishing*.

About the author

Sue's passionate relationship with books began when she was taught to read by her mum at three years old. So publishing as a career became the obvious choice for her in the early 1990s, after brief dabbles with the theatre and academia. Based in the young, dynamic, and super-creative city of Bristol, Sue now runs SRA Books, an independent publishing house offering book consultancy, production and trade distribution services to authors of all kinds from business owners to artists and designers to cooks.

Creating an imprint and resource especially for the ever-growing community of small business owners and business professionals has long been her dream and in May 2016 the first of the Authority Guides rolled off the press. Sue was so pleased with the result she decided to write the book you are holding in your hands in order to encourage more people to write, publish and market their own business books.

If you would like to find out more about working with Sue and her team, either as an independently published author of your own bespoke book project or as part of the Authority Guides, please do not hesitate to get in touch.

Email: admin@suerichardson.co.uk
Web: suerichardson.co.uk

EU Safety Representative: euComply OÜ Pärnu mnt 139b-14 11317 Tallinn
Estonia hello@eucompliancepartner.com +33 756 90241

www.ingramcontent.com/pod-product-compliance
Lightning Source LLC
LaVergne TN
LVHW021134160826
845679LV00016B/1744

* 9 7 8 1 9 0 9 1 1 6 7 9 5 *